EYEZ GIRAUD

Affiliate Marketing For Beginners

The Ultimate Guide To Earning Online

First edition

This book was professionally typeset on Reedsy.
Find out more at reedsy.com

This Book is dedicated to my Mother Gloria Toussaint-Giraud, my Father
Pattson Giraud
and my Grandmother Lucy.
Thank You, for all your love and support throughout my life.

"Impossible is a word to be found only in the dictionary of fools."

"History is the version of past events that people have decided to agree upon."

"Victory belongs to the most persevering."

"Courage isn't having the strength to go on—it is going on when you don't have strength."

NAPOLEON HILL
"

Contents

1

Table of Content

A ffiliate Marketing For Beginners :- The Ultimate Guide To Earning Online

Chapter 5 Finding and Joining Affiliate Programs

- Top affiliate networks and programs
- How to sign up and get approved

Chapter 6 Building Your Platform: Creating a Website or Blog

- Step-by-step guide to setting up a website
- Essential tools and plugins

Chapter 7 Content Creation Strategies: Blogging, Videos, and More

- Types of content that attract and convert
- Content planning and scheduling

Chapter 8 Email Marketing for Affiliate Success

- Building and growing an email list
- Crafting effective email campaigns

Chapter 9 Why It's Important to End Your Prices with a 7, 97, 5, or 95

Chapter 1: Introduction: Welcome to the World of Affiliate Marketing

Welcome to the world of Affiliate Marketing! In this book, we aim to guide you through the essentials of affiliate marketing, helping you navigate the path to earning money online. Whether you're a complete beginner or looking to refine your skills, this guide will provide you with the knowledge and tools to succeed.

Affiliate marketing is an exciting and dynamic way to generate income by promoting products or services and earning a commission for every sale or lead generated. This model benefits both merchants, who get increased sales, and affiliates, who earn a share of the revenue.

We will cover everything from the basics of affiliate marketing to advanced strategies for driving traffic and optimizing performance. By the end of this book, you'll have a comprehensive understanding of affiliate marketing and how to leverage it to achieve your financial goals.

Chapter 2: Why is Affiliate Marketing the Future of Business

Affiliate marketing is increasingly seen as the future of business, and here's why:

1. **Cost-Effectiveness:** Unlike traditional advertising, affiliate marketing allows businesses to pay only for actual performance, such as sales or leads. This makes it a cost-effective strategy, especially for small businesses and startups with limited marketing budgets.

2. **Scalability:** Affiliate marketing can easily scale as your business grows. By partnering with more affiliates, businesses can expand their reach and increase sales without significantly increasing costs.

3. **Global Reach:** With affiliates spread across the globe, businesses can reach international markets without the need for a physical presence in each country. This global reach is invaluable in today's interconnected world.

4. **Flexibility:** Affiliates have the flexibility to work from anywhere, promoting products they are passionate about.

This flexibility attracts a diverse range of affiliates, from bloggers and influencers to niche website owners.

5. **Performance-Based:** The performance-based nature of affiliate marketing ensures that marketing efforts are aligned with business goals. Affiliates are motivated to drive quality traffic and conversions, benefiting both parties.

6. **Trust and Credibility:** Affiliates often have established trust and credibility with their audience. When they recommend a product or service, their followers are more likely to trust the recommendation, leading to higher conversion rates.

Example 1: Cost-Effectiveness

Imagine a small business selling eco-friendly products. Instead of spending thousands of dollars on traditional advertising, they partner with eco-conscious bloggers and influencers who promote their products to a targeted audience. The business only pays a commission on actual sales, making their marketing spend highly efficient.

Example 2: Scalability

A fitness equipment company starts with a few affiliate partnerships. As the business grows, they onboard more fitness influencers, bloggers, and even gym owners as affiliates. This network of affiliates helps the company reach a wider audience without needing a proportional increase in their marketing budget.

Diagram: Affiliate Marketing Model

This diagram illustrates the basic affiliate marketing model, showing the flow from the merchant to the affiliate to the customer, and the commission earned on sales.

Chapter 3: Understanding the Basics: What is Affiliate Marketing?

Detailed Explanation of the Affiliate Marketing Process

A ffiliate marketing is a performance-based marketing strategy that benefits both businesses, referred to as merchants or advertisers, and their marketing partners, known as affiliates, publishers, or partners. In this symbiotic relationship, merchants gain additional customers and sales, while affiliates earn commissions for their marketing efforts. To understand the affiliate marketing process, it is essential to explore its detailed workings step-by-step.

The first step in the affiliate marketing process involves the merchant creating an affiliate program. The merchant sets up the program, clearly outlining its terms and conditions. These include the commission rates that affiliates can earn, the payment methods to be used, and the tracking systems that will monitor affiliate activities. Once the program is established, affiliates interested in promoting the merchant's products or services apply to join. Upon approval, they receive access to unique affiliate links and marketing materials designed to aid their promotional efforts.

Affiliates then begin promoting the merchant's products or services using various marketing strategies. These can include blogging, social media marketing, email campaigns, and paid advertising. The key is the use of unique affiliate links, which contain tracking codes that record the affiliate's ID and track the customer's activity on the merchant's website. When a potential customer clicks on an affiliate's unique link, they are directed to the merchant's site, and the tracking code ensures that any subsequent actions taken by the customer are attributed to the correct affiliate.

If the customer makes a purchase or completes a desired action, such as filling out a form, the affiliate is credited with a commission. The merchant tracks the sales and actions generated by each affiliate using the tracking systems put in place. After verifying the transactions, the merchant pays the affiliate their earned commission, thus completing the affiliate marketing cycle. This process benefits both parties: merchants achieve higher sales volumes without upfront advertising costs, and affiliates earn income based on their marketing effectiveness.

To delve deeper into affiliate marketing, it's crucial to understand some key terms. The merchant is the business or individual selling a product or service, also known as the advertiser or retailer. The affiliate is the individual or company promoting the merchant's product or service in exchange for a commission, also referred to as the publisher or partner. An affiliate network is a platform that connects merchants with affiliates, handling tracking, reporting, and payment processing. Examples include **ShareASale, CJ Affiliate,** and **Amazon Associates.** The commission is the payment an affiliate receives for driving a sale or specific action, which can be a fixed amount or a percentage of the sale. A tracking link is a unique URL provided to affiliates to track their marketing efforts, containing information that helps the merchant attribute sales or actions to the correct affiliate. Finally, a conversion is the desired action that the merchant wants the customer to take, such as making a purchase, signing up for a newsletter, or downloading an app.

There are various types of affiliate programs, each catering to different marketing strategies and goals. The most common type is the **Pay-Per-Sale (PPS) program,** where affiliates earn a commission each time they drive a sale. This model directly ties affiliate earnings to the sales performance, making it a popular choice for many merchants. Another type is the **Pay-Per-Click (PPC) program,** where affiliates earn a commission for each click they drive to the merchant's website, regardless of whether a sale is made. This model rewards affiliates for generating traffic, which can be particularly useful for brand awareness campaigns.

The Pay-Per-Lead (PPL) program is another variant where affiliates earn a commission for driving leads. This could involve actions such as customers filling out contact forms, signing up for free trials, or subscribing to newsletters. PPL programs are effective for businesses looking to build a list of potential customers or increase user engagement. Two-Tier Programs offer an added layer of earning potential by allowing affiliates to earn commissions not only for their own sales but also for sales generated by affiliates they recruit into the program. This model encourages affiliates to build networks of sub-affiliates, expanding the reach of the marketing effort.

Recurring Programs are designed for subscription-based products or services. Affiliates in these programs earn recurring commissions for as long as the customer remains subscribed, providing a steady stream of income over time. For example, an affiliate promoting a software subscription service might earn a commission every month the referred customer continues their subscription. Lastly, Lifetime Commissions programs offer affiliates the opportunity to earn a commission on all future purchases made by a customer they referred. This model incentivizes affiliates to build long-term relationships with customers, as they continue to benefit from repeat purchases.

In summary, affiliate marketing is a dynamic and effective strategy that leverages the strengths of both merchants and affiliates to drive sales and generate income. By understanding the affiliate marketing process, key terms, and various program types, businesses and marketers can effectively participate in and benefit from this powerful marketing approach. Whether through PPS, PPC, PPL, or other models, affiliate marketing offers diverse opportunities for revenue generation and business growth. By strategically implementing these programs, both merchants and affiliates can achieve their marketing goals and build lasting, profitable partnerships

Remember, success in affiliate marketing requires dedication, effective promotion strategies, and a good understanding of your audience. Whether you're a merchant looking to boost sales or an affiliate aiming to earn commissions, mastering the basics is the first step towards achieving your goals.

Chapter 4: Choosing the Right Niche: How to Find Profitable Markets

Finding the right niche is crucial to building a successful business. It involves identifying your interests and strengths, conducting market research, and analyzing competition. This chapter will guide you through these steps to ensure you choose a profitable niche.

Steps to Identify Your Interests and Strengths

1. **Self-Assessment**:

- **Interests**: List hobbies, activities, and topics you enjoy. Passion can drive motivation and perseverance.
- **Skills**: Identify your skills and expertise. Consider professional experience, educational background, and personal achievements.
- **Values**: Reflect on your values and what matters to you. A niche aligned with your values ensures long-term satisfaction.

2.**Brainstorming**:

- Combine your interests, skills, and values to create a list of potential niches. For instance, if you love cooking and have a background in nutrition, consider niches like healthy eating, meal planning, or culinary classes.

3.Validation:

- Share your niche ideas with friends, family, or mentors for feedback. Their perspectives can help refine your choices.

Conducting Market Research to Find Profitable Niches

4.Identify Market Demand:

- **Google Trends**: Use this tool to gauge the popularity of your niche over time. Look for consistent or growing interest.
- **Keyword Research**: Tools like Ubersuggest or Ahrefs can reveal search volumes for keywords related to your niche. High search volumes indicate strong demand.
- **Social Media**: Explore relevant groups, pages, and hashtags on platforms like Facebook, Instagram, and LinkedIn. High engagement levels suggest a thriving community.

5.Understand Your Audience:

- **Demographics**: Define the age, gender, location, and income level of your target audience. This helps tailor your products or services to their needs.
- **Pain Points**: Identify common problems or challenges faced by your audience. Online forums, reviews, and surveys are valuable sources of insights.

- **Preferences**: Understand their preferences, such as preferred content formats (blogs, videos, podcasts) and purchasing behaviors.

6.Market Size and Growth Potential:

- Assess the current size of your niche market. Is it large enough to support your business goals?
- Evaluate the growth potential. A niche with increasing interest and expanding audience base is ideal.

Analyzing Competition in Your Chosen Niche

7.Identify Competitors:

- Search for businesses and influencers in your niche. Note their products, services, and content strategies.
- Use tools like SEMrush or SimilarWeb to analyze their online presence and traffic sources.

8.Evaluate Their Strengths and Weaknesses:

- **Strengths**: Identify what they do well. This could be high-quality content, strong branding, or excellent customer service.
- **Weaknesses**: Look for gaps in their offerings, negative reviews, or areas where they lack expertise. These gaps are opportunities for you.

9.Differentiate Yourself:

- Determine your unique selling proposition (USP). What sets you apart from the competition? It could be a specialized service, innovative product, or a unique brand voice.

- Focus on delivering value that your competitors do not. This could be through superior customer service, exclusive content, or a niche-specific approach.

10.Monitor Competitor Activity:

- Keep an eye on your competitors' marketing strategies, new product launches, and customer engagement efforts. Staying informed helps you adapt and stay ahead.

By following these steps, you can confidently choose a niche that aligns with your passions, meets market demand, and stands out from the competition. A well-chosen niche is the foundation of a profitable and sustainable business.

This section provides a comprehensive and easy-to-follow guide on how to identify a profitable niche by focusing on personal interests and strengths, conducting thorough market research, and analyzing competition effectively.

6

Chapter 5: Finding and Joining Affiliate Programs

A ffiliate marketing is a powerful way to monetize your online presence. This chapter will guide you through the top affiliate networks and programs, the criteria for selecting the best ones, and tips for getting approved by these programs.

Overview of Top Affiliate Networks and Programs

1. **Amazon Associates**:

- One of the largest and most popular affiliate programs.
- Offers a wide range of products, making it easy to find items relevant to your niche.
- Commissions vary by product category.

2.**ShareASale**:

- A well-established network with a diverse range of merchants.
- Offers tools and resources to help affiliates succeed.

- Known for its reliability and timely payments.

3.CJ Affiliate (formerly Commission Junction):

- Provides access to many large brands and well-known companies.
- Advanced tracking and reporting tools.
- Requires a well-established website to join.

4.Rakuten Marketing:

- Connects affiliates with leading global brands.
- Offers a user-friendly interface and detailed performance reports.
- Focuses on quality over quantity of affiliates.

5.ClickBank:

- Specializes in digital products such as eBooks, online courses, and software.
- High commission rates compared to physical product affiliate programs.
- Ideal for niches like self-improvement, health, and online business.

6.Impact:

- Features a wide variety of brands, from small businesses to large corporations.
- Offers flexible partnership options and real-time tracking.
- Known for its transparent and efficient platform.

Criteria for Selecting the Best Programs

7.Relevance to Your Niche:

- Choose programs that offer products or services relevant to your audience.
- A strong match between your content and the affiliate products increases the likelihood of conversions.

8.Commission Rates:

- Evaluate the commission rates offered by different programs.
- Higher commissions can significantly increase your earnings, but balance this with the product's relevance and quality.

9.Cookie Duration:

- The length of time a cookie remains active is crucial. Longer cookie durations provide a greater chance of earning commissions from repeat visitors.
- Aim for programs offering at least a 30-day cookie duration.

10.Payment Terms:

- Check the payment frequency (monthly, bi-monthly) and methods (bank transfer, PayPal, check).
- Ensure the minimum payout threshold is achievable within a reasonable timeframe.

11.Support and Resources:

- Look for programs that offer robust support and resources, such as marketing materials, training, and dedicated affiliate managers.
- Good support can help you optimize your campaigns and increase earnings.

12.Reputation and Reliability:

- Research the program's reputation within the affiliate community.
- Reliable programs with a track record of timely payments and fair practices are essential for long-term success.

Tips for Getting Approved by Affiliate Programs

13.Professional Website:

- Ensure your website is professional, user-friendly, and relevant to the niche you're targeting.
- Quality content and a clear value proposition increase your chances of approval.

14.Clear Privacy Policy:

- A clear and comprehensive privacy policy shows that you take your visitors' data seriously.
- Many affiliate programs require this as part of their compliance standards.

15.Consistent Traffic:

- Demonstrate consistent traffic to your website. Most programs prefer affiliates with a steady flow of visitors.

- Use analytics tools to provide accurate traffic data if requested.

16.Quality Content:

- Produce high-quality, original content that engages your audience.
- Highlight how you plan to promote the affiliate products within your content.

17.Social Media Presence:

- A strong social media presence can bolster your application.
- Share your social media stats and engagement metrics if they are impressive.

18.Application Details:

- Provide detailed and honest information in your application.
- Explain why you're a good fit for the program and how you plan to promote their products.

Buy carefully selecting affiliate programs and following these tips for approval, you can build a successful affiliate marketing strategy. A strong network of affiliate partnerships can significantly boost your revenue and help you grow your online business.

This section provides a comprehensive guide on finding and joining affiliate programs, focusing on key factors such as network overviews, selection criteria, and application tips.

Chapter 6: Building Your Platform: Creating a Website or Blog

C reating a website or blog is a crucial step in establishing your online presence. This chapter will guide you through choosing a domain name and web hosting service, setting up your website step-by-step, and essential tools and plugins for optimization.

Choosing a Domain Name and Web Hosting Service

1. **Choosing a Domain Name**:

- **Relevance**: Ensure your domain name reflects your brand or niche. It should be intuitive and convey the essence of your content.
- **Simplicity**: Keep it simple and easy to remember. Avoid complex words, hyphens, or numbers which can confuse visitors.
- **Keywords**: Incorporate relevant keywords if possible. This can help with search engine optimization (SEO).
- **Availability**: Check the availability of your desired domain name. Use tools like Namecheap or GoDaddy to see if it's taken and explore

alternatives if necessary.

- **Extensions**: Opt for popular extensions like .com, .net, or .org. These are generally more trusted and recognized by users.

2.Choosing a Web Hosting Service:

- **Reliability and Uptime**: Choose a hosting service with a proven track record of reliability and high uptime (99.9% or above).
- **Speed**: Fast loading times are crucial for user experience and SEO. Look for hosts with good performance metrics.
- **Support**: Opt for providers offering 24/7 customer support. Issues can arise at any time, and responsive support is vital.
- **Scalability**: As your site grows, your hosting needs may change. Choose a service that can scale with your growth.
- **Security**: Ensure the host offers robust security features like SSL certificates, firewalls, and regular backups.
- **Popular Options**: Some reliable web hosting services include Bluehost, SiteGround, and HostGator.

Step-by-Step Guide to Setting Up a Website

3.Register Your Domain:

- Use a domain registrar like Namecheap, GoDaddy, or Google Domains to register your chosen domain name.
- Follow the registration process, provide necessary details, and complete the purchase.

4.Select and Purchase a Hosting Plan:

- Choose a hosting plan that suits your needs. Shared hosting is suitable for beginners, while VPS or dedicated hosting is better for high-traffic sites.

- Complete the signup process with your chosen hosting provider.

5.Connect Your Domain to Your Hosting:

- Access your hosting account and find the domain settings.
- Update the DNS (Domain Name System) settings to point your domain to your hosting provider's servers.

6.Install a Content Management System (CMS):

- **WordPress**: The most popular CMS, known for its flexibility and ease of use.
- Log into your hosting account, navigate to the control panel, and use the one-click WordPress installer.

7.Choose and Install a Theme:

- Access the WordPress dashboard and go to "Appearance" > "Themes".
- Browse free themes or purchase a premium theme from market-places like ThemeForest.
- Install and activate your chosen theme.

8.Customize Your Website:

- Go to "Appearance" > "Customize" to adjust the theme settings, such as colors, fonts, and layout.
- Create essential pages like Home, About, Contact, and Blog.

9.Install Essential Plugins:

- Plugins add functionality to your site. Some must-have plugins include:
- **Yoast SEO**: For optimizing your site for search engines.
- **Jetpack**: For security, performance, and site management tools.
- **WPForms**: For creating contact forms.

10.Create and Publish Content:

- Start creating blog posts or pages relevant to your niche.
- Use a content calendar to plan and schedule your posts regularly.

Essential Tools and Plugins for Optimization

11.SEO Tools:

- **Yoast SEO**: Helps optimize your content for search engines with easy-to-follow guidelines.
- **Google Analytics**: Tracks and reports website traffic, providing insights into user behavior.
- **Google Search Console**: Monitors your site's presence in Google search results and helps identify issues.

12.Performance Optimization:

- **WP Super Cache**: Improves site speed by creating static versions of your pages.
- **Smush**: Compresses and optimizes images to reduce loading times.
- **Autoptimize**: Aggregates and minifies scripts and styles to enhance performance.

13.Security:

- **Wordfence Security**: Provides robust security features including firewall protection and malware scanning.
- **Sucuri Security**: Offers comprehensive security measures and monitoring.
- **UpdraftPlus**: Backs up your site and allows for easy restoration.

14.User Experience:

- **Elementor**: A drag-and-drop page builder that simplifies website design.
- **WPForms**: An easy-to-use form builder for creating contact forms, surveys, and more.
- **MonsterInsights**: Integrates Google Analytics with WordPress, making it easy to view your analytics data within the dashboard.

By following these steps and utilizing the right tools and plugins, you can create a professional, optimized, and secure website or blog. This will provide a solid foundation for your online business and help you effectively engage with your audience.

Chapter 7: Content Creation Strategies: Blogging, Videos, and More

C reating compelling content is vital for attracting and retaining your audience. In this chapter, we delve into the essentials of blogging, video creation, and promoting your content effectively. The strategies outlined here will help you engage your audience, build trust, and establish a strong online presence.

Writing Compelling Blog Posts and Creating Engaging Videos

1. Blog Posts:

Creating captivating blog posts starts with a strong headline. Your headline is the first thing readers see, so it must grab their attention immediately. Consider using numbers, questions, or strong adjectives to make your headline stand out. For instance, a headline like "10 Proven Ways to Increase Your Blog Traffic" is likely to attract more readers than a generic one.

The introduction of your blog post is equally crucial. Hook your readers within the first few sentences by stating a problem they can relate to and promising a solution. This approach not only grabs attention but also sets the stage for delivering valuable content. For example, an introduction that starts with "Are you struggling to get more visitors to your blog? In this post, we'll share ten proven strategies to boost your traffic and keep your audience engaged."

The body of your blog post should provide valuable information presented in an easy-to-read format. Use subheadings, bullet points, and images to break up the text and enhance readability. Each section should flow logically, ensuring that your readers can follow your arguments and insights without getting lost. Providing real-life examples, case studies, or data can add credibility to your content.

Concluding your blog post with a summary of the key points and a call-to-action (CTA) is essential. The CTA could be an invitation to leave a comment, share the post, or check out related content. For example, "In summary, these ten strategies can significantly increase your blog traffic. Try implementing them and let us know your results in the comments below."

2.Videos:

Creating engaging videos requires careful planning and execution. Start with a well-thought-out script that keeps the content concise and engaging. A clear script helps you stay focused and ensures that your message is delivered effectively. Just like with blog posts, including a CTA in your video script is crucial. Encourage viewers to like, share, comment, or subscribe to your channel.

When it comes to production, the quality of your video matters. Good lighting, clear audio, and steady filming are the basics that you must get right. Investing in a decent microphone and camera can make a significant difference. Additionally, using editing software like Adobe Premiere or iMovie can enhance your video by adding professional touches, such as transitions, text overlays, and background music.

To boost engagement, encourage viewers to interact with your content. Ask them to leave comments, likes, and shares. Responding to viewer feedback shows that you value their input and fosters a sense of community around your content. For example, you could say, "Let us know in the comments what you think about these tips, and don't forget to like and share this video if you found it helpful."

Planning and Scheduling Content for Maximum Impact

3.Content Calendar:

A content calendar is an indispensable tool for any content creator. Planning your posts and videos in advance helps you maintain consistency and organization. It also allows you to align your content with important dates and events relevant to your niche. For example, if you're a fitness blogger, you might plan content around major marathons or health awareness months.

Creating a content calendar involves mapping out what content you'll publish and when. This approach ensures that you always have fresh content ready to go, reducing last-minute stress and improving the quality of your work. Tools like Google Calendar, Trello, or dedicated content calendar software can help you stay organized.

4.Frequency:

Consistency is key when it comes to content creation. Aim for regular posting schedules, such as one blog post per week and one video bi-weekly. This frequency keeps your audience engaged and coming back for more. However, it's essential to balance quality with quantity. Posting too often at the expense of quality can lead to disengagement. It's better to have fewer high-quality posts or videos than a plethora of mediocre ones.

Leveraging Social Media to Promote Your Content

5.Platforms:

Choosing the right social media platforms to promote your content is crucial. Identify where your audience is most active and focus your efforts there. For example, if your target audience is young adults, platforms like Instagram and TikTok might be more effective than Facebook. Conversely, if you're targeting professionals, LinkedIn could be a better fit.

Each platform has its own strengths and best practices, so tailor your approach accordingly. For instance, Instagram is great for visually appealing content, while Twitter is ideal for sharing quick updates and engaging in conversations.

6.Promotion:

Promoting your content on social media involves more than just sharing links. Craft compelling descriptions that entice your audience to click through and engage with your content. Use relevant hashtags to increase visibility and reach a broader audience. For example, if you're sharing a blog post about digital marketing, hashtags like #DigitalMarketing, #SEO, and #ContentCreation can help attract the right audience.

Engagement is a two-way street. Respond to comments and messages promptly to build relationships with your audience. Show appreciation for their feedback and use it to improve your future content. For example, if a viewer asks a question or leaves a suggestion, acknowledge it and consider incorporating it into your next post or video.

In conclusion, creating compelling content involves a strategic approach to blogging, video production, and promotion. By writing attention-grabbing blog posts, producing high-quality videos, and leveraging social media effectively, you can attract and retain a loyal audience. Planning your content in advance and maintaining a consistent posting schedule are key factors in achieving long-term success. Engaging with your audience and responding to their feedback will further strengthen your online presence and build a community around your content.

Chapter 8: Email Marketing for Affiliate Success

E mail marketing is a powerful tool for building relationships with your audience and driving sales for your affiliate marketing efforts. It allows you to communicate directly with your subscribers, providing them with valuable content, updates, and offers that can lead to conversions. To harness the full potential of email marketing, you need to focus on strategies for building and growing your email list, crafting effective email campaigns, and automating your email marketing efforts.

Strategies for Building and Growing an Email List

The foundation of a successful email marketing strategy is a robust and engaged email list. Building and growing this list requires enticing incentives and strategic placement of sign-up forms. One effective method to encourage sign-ups is offering opt-in incentives. Freebies such as eBooks, checklists, or discounts are powerful motivators for visitors to subscribe to your email list. These incentives should be relevant to your niche and valuable enough to prompt immediate action. For instance, if you run a fitness blog, offering a free eBook on "10 Effective Home Workouts" can attract fitness enthusiasts to join your mailing list.

Equally important is the placement of sign-up forms. These forms should be prominently displayed on your website, blog, and social media channels. An eye-catching sign-up form on your homepage, a pop-up form after a certain time on your blog, or a link in your social media bios can significantly increase your subscription rates. Ensure that the forms are easy to fill out and require minimal information, typically just a name and email address, to reduce friction and improve sign-up rates.

Automating Your Email Marketing Efforts

To maximize efficiency and maintain consistency, automate your email marketing efforts using email automation tools. Platforms like Mailchimp, ConvertKit, and others offer features that allow you to set up automated email sequences and manage your campaigns effortlessly. These tools enable you to schedule emails, segment your audience, and track the performance of your campaigns, freeing up time to focus on other aspects of your business.

One of the most effective ways to use automation is through drip campaigns. Drip campaigns are automated series of emails that nurture subscribers over time. These sequences can introduce new subscribers to your brand, provide valuable content, and ultimately drive conversions. For instance, a new subscriber might receive a welcome email, followed by a series of educational emails about your niche, and finally, a few emails promoting your affiliate products. Each email in the sequence should build on the previous one, gradually moving the subscriber closer to making a purchase.

Chapter 9: Why It's Important to End Your Prices with a 7, 97, 5, or 95

P ricing strategies can significantly impact consumer behavior and sales.

Psychological Pricing Strategies

Examples of Effective Pricing in Affiliate Marketing

1. Pricing strategies play a crucial role in influencing consumer behavior and driving sales. One of the most effective tactics in this realm is psychological pricing, which leverages the way consumers perceive and react to prices. Understanding and implementing these strategies can significantly enhance your marketing efforts and boost your conversions. This chapter explores the nuances of psychological pricing, particularly the impact of ending prices with specific digits like 7, 97, 5, or 95, and provides practical examples of their effectiveness in affiliate marketing.

Psychological Pricing Strategies

2.Psychological pricing strategies are designed to create a perception of value and affordability, often leading to increased sales. One of the most popular techniques is charm pricing, which involves setting prices that end in 7, 97, 5, or 95. This approach is based on the idea that consumers perceive these prices as better deals compared to rounded figures. For instance, a product priced at $9.97 appears significantly cheaper than one priced at $10, even though the difference is only three cents. This small change can have a substantial impact on the consumer's purchasing decision, making the product seem more attractive and affordable.

3.Charm pricing works because consumers tend to process prices from left to right. When they see $9.97, their brain registers the $9 first, which is associated with a lower price range than $10. This effect, known as the left-digit effect, makes the price seem smaller and more appealing. Additionally, prices ending in 7 or 5 are less common than those ending in 0 or 9, which can make them stand out and appear more distinctive. This subtle difference can enhance the perceived value of the product and increase the likelihood of a purchase.

Examples of Effective Pricing in Affiliate Marketing

4.To illustrate the effectiveness of charm pricing, we can look at several case studies in affiliate marketing. Many marketers have found that adjusting their prices to end in 7, 97, 5, or 95 can lead to higher conversion rates. For example, an affiliate marketer promoting a digital product priced at $29.97 might see a significant boost in sales compared to pricing the same product at $30. Similarly, a price of $14.95 for a physical product might outperform a $15 price point in terms of conversions and overall sales volume. These real-world examples highlight the power of charm pricing in influencing consumer behavior and driving sales.

5.Testing different price points is another essential aspect of optimizing your pricing strategy. Every audience is unique, and what works for one group may not work for another. Conducting A/B tests with various price endings can help you determine the most effective pricing for your target market. For instance, you might test a price of $19.97 against $19.95 and $20 to see which one generates the highest conversion rate. By analyzing the results, you can gain valuable insights into your audience's preferences and adjust your pricing strategy accordingly.

6.Encouraging experimentation with different price points is crucial for finding the optimal strategy for your products or services. Regularly testing and refining your pricing can help you stay competitive and maximize your revenue. It's important to track the performance of each pricing variation and consider factors such as the overall sales volume, profit margins, and customer feedback. This iterative approach ensures that you are continuously improving and adapting to market trends and consumer behavior.

7.In conclusion, understanding and implementing psychological pricing strategies can significantly impact your affiliate marketing success. Charm pricing, which involves ending prices with 7, 97, 5, or 95, leverages the way consumers perceive prices and can make products seem more affordable and appealing. Real-world examples and case studies demonstrate the effectiveness of this approach in increasing conversions and driving sales. Additionally, testing different price points is essential for finding the most effective pricing strategy for your audience. By continuously refining your approach and leveraging psychological pricing, you can enhance your marketing efforts, attract more customers, and ultimately boost your affiliate marketing success.

Conclusion

In conclusion, "Affiliate Marketing For Beginners: The Ultimate Guide To Earning Online" equips you with the essential knowledge and strategies to embark on your affiliate marketing journey. By understanding the fundamental principles, key terms, and various types of affiliate programs, you can make informed decisions and create effective marketing campaigns. The detailed explanations and practical tips provided in this book empower you to build a solid foundation, leverage different marketing channels, and continuously optimize your efforts. With dedication, persistence, and a focus on creating value for your audience, you can turn affiliate marketing into a lucrative online income stream. Remember, success in affiliate marketing comes from continuous learning, adapting to market trends, and consistently delivering high-quality content to your audience.

For additional information on how to make money in Affiliate Marketing go to www.coacheyez.com

To join. my community go to https://www.pxcommunity.coacheyez.com

Resources

Instant Income by Janet Switzer: Strategies that bring in the cash for small businesses, innovative employees and entrepreneurs. (2007). The McGraw Hill Companies. https://www.instantincome.com

Brunson, R. (2020). Expert secrets: The Underground Playbook for Converting Your Online Visitors into Lifelong Customers. Hay House, Inc.

Magnetic Marketing: How to attract a flood of new customers that pay, stay

and refer. (2018). Forbesbooks. https://MagneticMarketing.com